TO MY BELOVED MOTHER, MARIA

Blessed Kearns

Published by New Generation Publishing in 2023 Copyright ©
BLESSED KEARNS 2023

First Edition

The author asserts the moral right under the Copyright, Designs and Patents Act 1988 to be identified as the author of this work.

All Rights reserved. No part of this publication may be reproduced, stored in a retrieval system or transmitted, in any form or by any means without the prior consent of the author, nor be otherwise circulated in any form of binding or cover other than that which it is published and without a similar condition being imposed on the subsequent purchaser.

ISBN
Paperback: 978-1-80369-866-3
Hardback: 978-1-80369-874-8
Ebook: 978-1-80369-875-5

www.newgeneration-publishing.com
New Generation Publishing

This book is in honour of my beloved mother, Maria, and the memories that I have of her while I was growing up and the times we shared together. Some of the memories that I hold are sad, as well as happy times, and I will be reflecting on some of the endeavours that I have faced and some of the proudest moments of my life. For instance, being a student at Wolverhampton University, graduating in 2006 as a registered Mental Health Nurse.

Everything I have achieved in my life so far has been so with perseverance. I was not born with a silver spoon in my mouth, and I have had to raise my children as a single parent.

This book is also dedicated to the woman who brought me to this world; she worked very hard to raise nine children with no immediate family members to support her (my grandmother, siblings etc.) and it is Maria with less support. But when I look back, I have come to realise that at least you did not suffer and you were not bedbound, but still, I never got that chance to say goodbye. Never would I have imagined that you would have gone from my life so soon; you were too young to die, and I thought you would still be here today. But I was wrong. I feel so guilty because I never made it to your funeral, Mom, but I was unable to. Some things are beyond our control, but nevertheless, I will always hate myself for it.

My beloved mother loved me unconditionally and had so much care and empathy for her children, like a chicken, hiding its chick from the hungry wild animals. I loved my mother. She taught me to be who I am today, and I am extremely proud of her. I have learned to take the negative thoughts and turn them into positive ones, which is what drove me to write this biography. I have reflected on certain events that happened to me as a child, when I would fetch a container of water and carry it on my head for a long distance, over several trips.

When I look back, I have realised now (as a mother as well) what she must have gone through. My mother's passing was sudden and hurts to this day. However, from what my siblings have told me, she was complaining of chest pains, which resulted in her having a fatal heart attack. I comfort myself in knowing that your passing was sudden and that your pain was not elongated.

Your voice echoes in my head all the time; you mentioned that at some point I will not find you there, and now I know you were right. I will not find you, Mom. There is something about losing your mother that is permanent.

"You will lose someone you can't live without, and your heart will be badly broken, and the bad news is that you never completely get over the loss of your beloved.

They live forever in your broken heart that doesn't seal back up. There is also the good news of keeping those memories in a hidden box in your heart and the only person who has the key to that box is you,

My mother had less support, as most of her family were in South Africa. I presume this must have been extremely hard for her, but she stayed with us. When I look back, I realise how lucky I was to have her as my mother, and I knew deep-down that I was loved, and I felt it. You left too soon although you did not suffer, Mom, and you will always be remembered by me for your courage, your strength, your love for your children, and your kindness by accommodating our neighbours when they needed you. Whether it was the little essentials, e.g., salt, sugar or cooking oil, you shared this.

As the saying goes: *"Don't be ashamed to weep; 'tis right to grieve. Tears are only water, and flowers, trees, and fruit cannot grow without water. But there must be sunlight also. A wounded heart will heal in time, and when it does, the memory and love of our lost ones is sealed inside to comfort us."* – Brian Jacques, *Taggerung*.

I know I am not alone when I say your voice echoes in my head constantly, because others have also said, When you mentioned to me at some point that I will not find you there, and you were right. I won't see you or would be able talk, to let you know what I have accomplished and archived through determination and issues I have endured. You were my mother, and I will always be your daughter, and I felt loved by you. *"There are wounds that never show on the body that are deeper and more hurtful than anything that bleeds."* – Laurell K. Hamilton, *Mistral's Kiss.*

"We need to find God, and he cannot be found in noise and restlessness. God is the friend of silence. Nature— trees, flowers, grass—grows in silence; see the stars, the moon and the sun, how they move in silence. We need silence to be able to touch souls." – Mother Teresa.

My mother was a very strong woman, both mentally and physically, and therefore her passing away was very difficult to accept. As we all know, we grieve in different ways. We all go through painful emotions. I loved my mother, and yet I feel I did not show her enough love when she was alive. I will always be immensely proud of her. She looked after me when I was a child, listened to my cries when I was hungry, and cleaned me when I was soiled. She was my mother. As a young girl my mother taught me a lot; that I needed be kind to people, and to give them food if they did not have enough, and to share whatever I had. Although we had very little growing up, we always shared food.

The nice part about growing up in the village was that there was so much to do; there were never any dull moments. At times when there were good rains, we could have watermelon, and there were wild fruits to eat. When there was no rain, the elderly believed beer had to be brewed, and there was a lot traditional dancing around a specific tree. Young girls were picked to travel to other villages. They were mostly naked from the top, but nobody was allowed to watch them. These girls were given a special name for this, but I was not one of them. They were told to carry branches from a certain tree with them, then the elders could do traditional dancing around this tree late in the afternoon for the rain to come. It seems so long ago, I remember very little about it now.

There were good and bad times when I was growing up. I have done bad things in the past, which I am not proud of, but I did not commit any murder. These memories will remain with me for the rest of my life. I struggled for a long time to forgive my father, and even though those wounds have healed slightly, it has been difficult for me. But I have, and as such, I feel much closer to God.

I did not attend secondary school, but I was able to go to university. I am still proud to work for the National Health Service (NHS), which I call a ~~bid industry~~ as it is multicultural. I have attended Dudley College while working at the same time, making myself available to pick up a few shifts here and there, which paid enough to put food on the table as well as buy my children some new clothes.

Having only attended primary school, I later went on to pass my NVQ Level 2 and 3 in Nursing, which was enough to get me accepted into university. I can recall doubting myself, wondering how I had managed to get this far when I was not as educated as some of the other students who had made it to university. Still, I was able to gain higher grades than many of those students, something that my mother would have been most proud of had she still been alive.

I can recall walking to the library and then having to get the bus home carrying a number of books because I did not have a car. I used to get a bus and then catch a train to Wolverhampton University, which I attended Monday to Friday, unless it was a bank holiday. I would do as many shifts as I could, always grateful for the opportunity to work for the NHS.

I would like to leave my legacy for my children and my grandchildren. I would also like to say that no matter how difficult the situation is, there is always a light and a door waiting for you to open. This is my biography, which is dedicated to the woman who brought me into this world: Maria, my beloved mother.

I grew up in Africa, which was a difficult upbringing, but one that has provided me with so many reasons to appreciate the person who I have turned into. As a child, I did not value the beauty of my homeland, its wilderness, and the wild animals that roamed the land.

This is Africa untamed; the land where I grew up. Africa is a beautiful continent, which has many tourist attractions, including the statue of David Livingstone by the Victoria Falls. The statue is situated by the river, which is full of crocodiles, and are known to eat humans who fall into the river. There is also a rainbow and a place where there is always water dripping down the stones of Mosi-oa-Tunya, which can be very slippery. There is also a game of rafting and sightseeing experiences like the helicopter rides over the Victoria Falls, where you can see the many animals roaming and even feeding. There are also nice fruits, which include sweet mangoes and watermelons.

People are very friendly there, but also quite poor. Normally, they sell their crops when they have harvested or sell watermelons if there have been good rains. It's a place which is very nice, especially when it rains. This benefits the villagers, allowing the people to grow their own crops, such as maize, watermelons, etc. Growing up in that environment made me a stronger person.

Mom, your voice echoes in my head all the time; when you said that at some point I will not find you there, now I know you were right.

I used to be friendly with another girl in the village; we were inseparable. We used to go and fetch firewood from the forest. As girls, we did a lot of house chores but we did not live together. She lived in the next village; we used to do a lot of things together, and there were some boys who had shown some interest in us. We would look forward to meeting up with them as they would help us fetch the water back to the village. We could fetch water even if others were not allowed to, as time had to be afforded to allow the cows to drink from the borehole. Collecting water required a lot of physical work, pushing the pump to bring gallons and gallons of the water out from the ground. For those that were fortunate this tedious chore was made easy when carts with 50l drums were pulled by donkeys.

After completing all my chores there were times when I would look after the cows. It was important to make sure that the cows did not wander off into other people's fields, or else you could get into trouble. My father had donkeys and a cart that was used to carry maize that was already dry from the fields and bring it home. I used to walk to school with no shoes, which was more difficult when it was wintertime. The school was quite far from the village and we used to travel barefoot, even if it was cold. I used to walk with other children from the village even if we were in different classes to one another. Most of the time we would go to school feeling very hungry. Some children would have pocket money and go to the shop near the school grounds and buy a small packet of biscuits, which sometimes they would share. Other children would carry boiled maize, which they would carry to school and then hide in the bushes. It would be covered in ants by the time they returned to collect it. You would have to pick it up and then blow off the ants before eating it. My father would never allow me to take anything to school; if I did, I would be in so much trouble.

In our village there was this man well known for sexually abusing his own children. Most of the villagers knew about this; it was a horrible thing to do, and nobody did anything about it. It was exceedingly difficult that he was allowed to get away with this, and he seemed to enjoy it, even though they were his children.

At times we used to go and meet other children from

the village and play when there was a full moon; we used to pretend we were adults. Sometimes there would be a fire and we would gather around it, but it was not in my village. While the adults were not supposed to know about this, they knew anyway. We were African children and we enjoyed being children. Kids play hide and seek, and this is what we did during the night; sit around the fire and pick up a piece of coal, moving it around and letting the others guess where it was, or play hide and seek. These were wonderful times and I wish I could go back to being young once again with no bills to pay.

I loved my young carefree life as our basic care used natural resources around use such as using sticks as toothbrushes. We never had any toothpaste or toothbrushes, so we used to use a tree bug to brush our teeth.

My father made me grow up too fast and made things ridiculously difficult, even unbearable for a long time. There was no remorse for what he did; he would just start shouting and this led to physical violence, which was mainly aimed towards me. He would be shouting and then he would lash out and start hitting me or my mother for no major reasons at all, and I really hated him for that. My father never showed his affection or love towards his children, but I could tell he loved my other siblings more than me.

There were events that happened during his violence which are not easy to forget. Although my father was not a big man, there were times when he presented a man possessed, without being provoked by anything. I can say this with a clear conscience.

His brutality and spitefulness were so severe that one cannot even imagine it. My father did little to deserve the family he had. I can recall one day an argument of some sort that had contributed to his anger. My father pinned my mother down on the floor. I was not sure when it started or what had started it, but he was sitting on her on the kitchen floor with his hands around her throat. Fortunately, there were no pots on the fire, but there was still burning wood, as we used to leave the fire burning until the logs had burned completely to keep ourselves warm.

I remember my father sitting on my mother when I walked into the kitchen and his eyes were blazing with anger. He was drunk at that particular time; I glanced at him and I saw his eyes bulging out of their sockets and blazing with fury. He had his hands around her throat, and she kept begging him to leave her alone. *"You are hurting me, you are hurting me… can you not see you are hurting me?"* She called out to him. I felt helpless as I watched him hold her down. I was a child after all, and this was exceedingly difficult.

I remember just going to find anything to hit him with, but I could not find anything. As a child, I was very frightened of him due to his violence, and by now, my mother's arm right arm was pinned to the fire. He was sitting on her and she could not move. He was deliberately burning her. I heard my mother calling him, so I walked back to the kitchen with a log I had found outside.

He glanced at me but I did not care. For the first time I was not scared of him; I knew something had to be done. I knew that once he got off my mother, he would turn on me. *So many times I wished that she could leave him but she did not; she stood by us.*

This is not something you would ever want to see; the wounds were very deep. I hated him for it. I felt helpless. I turned around, tears running down my cheeks, and hit him as hard as I could, but he just looked at me with his blazing eyes full of anger. I was crying very loud. After doing that I ran to the fields as fast as I could.

I do not know how others knew about this. I cannot remember whether we spoke about this, but there was so much anger and it frightened us so we met by the fields and tried to find a place to sleep. We found a place under the small bushes; we scrambled together using the same blankets for us to sleep. Thank the Lord we avoided the mosquitoes and the heavy rain. Only one of us needed to return to the village to get blankets for us to sleep. I cannot remember who did this, but we were all familiar with the field and had a name for it. If someone had mentioned the name of that field, you would know exactly where it was. One could just cross the road to get to the field.

At night the sky was clear enough to see the stars and the Milky Way, which I used to see frequently. As I looked up, I felt very angry, thinking about the whereabouts of my mother and wondering if she had survived her ordeal. During the night it drizzled a little bit, and I don't think we slept at all.

There were so many stars and even shooting stars that covered the night sky. There were no streetlights, only the moon and kerosene lamps to enable us to see. We would meet up with children from other villages to play during the night, which was fun.

We could stay for a long time without going to fetch water from the borehole. This water was helpful as we used it to cook and do the dishes, wash clothes and have baths. When there was so much water these were happy times, and it was nice as the work was not so difficult to do. *Happy times.* But still, the thought of my abusive father lingered with me.

There were times when we could stand outside when it was dark and have a bath. There was so much water due to the rains, which was extremely good for the crops and wildlife. That was village life. It was nice to be so carefree as children. We were happy, even sleeping together on the floor with my other siblings and sharing the same blankets; it was okay. It was girls. But they were younger than me. We could play in the rain running around naked; there was so much laughter, although my mother was against this, as she believed we could be struck by lightning. Now when look back, I think she was right; lightning can strike people.

There were times when the fire was made in the kitchen due to heavy rains and then it would get very smokey inside. There were no windows, so we needed to open the kitchen door, but not for long. The fire used to catch up very quickly and in wintertime it could get very cold. During the summer months, the fire was mainly to cook food, as we did not have any stoves. When it rained it was easier, as we had gutters that could collect water; if I recall they would fill up very quickly.

We used to look forward to the Christmas period; we had the luxury of getting new clothes and would scrub ourselves more than on other days. We were also told if we woke up early and made our trip to fetch water, we would see the sun dancing up in the sky. We were made to believe this, although we did not make a big issue as Christmas had finally arrived.

During this time the music was deafening and the children from other villages used to come to my village to dance and eat. Village people would come to my village where they would be given food, and my mother used to prepare home-brewed beer for the adults. Everyone would be enjoying themselves and the adults would be sitting under the trees, drinking the beer that had been brewed by my beloved mother. My mother was a very kind and gentle soul. She was exceptionally clean and particular with everything. When I reflect, I know that I was incredibly lucky to have her as my mother.

When it was hot, there were many flies, which often fell in jars of milk. Milk was difficult to get as we did not have too many cows, and the milk was left for the calves or to cook dry vegetables, which would have been picked from the fields and kept dry. I was not allowed to milk a cow, but of course, I could milk a goat. That was a privilege. At times I could pick up the cows' dung and mix this with water and smear it all over the kitchen floor. Once dry, I would sweep the floor clean using a grass sweeping broom, which used to be done once a week, usually on the weekend.

There were lots of wild fruits in the forest, for example, umkhemeswane, ubhunzu, umkojombo, unviyo, and amalolo, which were very nice. Even the caterpillars would eat them. As well as these African fruits, wild mushrooms grew in the forest, which were so easy to pick up.

I learned how to swim when the rains came, and we would make little boats by using the reeds that would grow by the valley. Depending on how many there were of us, we used to urge each to get on the boat, and we had a lot of fun doing so. We were children, carefree, and we enjoyed each other's company. I knew which children came from which village and we were a very close-knit community; this included the older people as well, who we had so much respect for. We were not allowed to give older people direct eye contact; if you did, you were viewed as a child with no manners and your parents would be informed.

There were scorpions and snakes, which I feared, but there were no lions nearby. At times we would get the opportunity of using clay to build cows, and then pretend that they were fighting each other; it was symbolic and fun, and regardless of being hungry, we still had a chance to play outside when it was raining. We could run around naked in the rain, although my mother was against this due to the risk of lightning. We smiled even though we could be struck by lightning. There was so much laughter.

Once it had stopped raining and the sun came out, so would these strange pink and fluffy insects that were bigger than ticks and would crawl around. They didn't stay out for long, and it was a mystery to us all as to where they came from, although we suspected it was from the ground. They were so delicate. Once we tried to pick them up, but they just died in our hands and we were told not to touch them again, as they belonged to God. But they were so pretty; they looked like ticks and they used to disappear very quickly. "*Izinja zikha nkulukhu.*" Presumably they got this name due to being so fragile.

But thoughts of my father never left me. He could go and travel with his scorecards to sell dry wood and watermelons, and he would stay away from the village when all was good. *"Mamba eyenyukile umucakide bucelesile."* In simple English, "When the cat is away the mice play."

When someone in authority is not present, those subordinate to that authority do whatever they want. If I leave my classroom for a moment and then I come back to find the place in chaos; when the cat's away, the mice will play. Without the correct supervision, children (or people) will do as they please—especially in disregarding or breaking the rules. For example, as soon as parents have left the house, then the children will invite all their friends over. That is how it was for us. Our father was never around.

I had a friend from the village and we used to get along fine; we lived close to each other, we used to fetch water and play together, and we understood each other. Her parents believed that giving her an education was not necessary, therefore she was not given chance to go to school. Regardless of that, she was my friend. I found living in the village extremely hard, but when my father was not there it made things easier. Although we were not rich, we got by. I was good in school, although I struggled when it came to maths. I was a good runner, although it was difficult running on an empty stomach. I used to play netball and perform school plays, which I was particularly good at. I was mainly chosen for small dramatic plays in school.

Doing jobs was necessary whether you liked it or not—it had to be done. I remember when I used to go fetch water by carrying a 5-gallon container full of water on my head, which would be done over several trips, over quite a distance from the village. This worried some of my neighbours as I was only short, and it was a lot of weight for me to carry.

I used to go to the bush and get a ~~mud~~ toothbrush stick to clean my teeth; I would chew the bud first, then spit out the bitter juice, and then clean my teeth. We did not have any toothbrushes or toothpaste, so we depended on that, which was very good. That was village life and we made ends meet, regardless of the situation.

There was this plant called inkunzane, which was a perfect shampoo that we used to use to wash our hair. This would grow in the valley and only when we had good rains.

We survived by ploughing, which is where most of our food came from. I could kill a chicken, a simple source of meat, yet it's something I don't think I could do now. Chicken eggs were not allowed to be eaten; if we dared touch those eggs, you knew there would be trouble. We needed the chicks to grow to be chickens for meat purposes.

My father broke my heart so many times, and I found it so hard to forgive him. He believed I was not his child, and that hurt me so much. He showed his love for my other siblings, even though there were a few occasions when he would be violent with them. But he was very cruel, especially with me, which proved to be more than I could take. It was peaceful when he was not around; he would go to places to sell watermelons and logs for fires to make money. But on his return home, he would be drunk.

We had maize which we used to grow in the fields, and at times when the corn was still soft, we could boil it and put it on the fire to have roasted corn, which was very nice.

Early one morning I had a feeling my mother must have left home, so I decided to try and find her. I knew there and then that if I really wanted to find her, I needed to start early, as there would be wild animals moving around and I would not be able to track her footprints. In addition, there were no clear roads in the village, and it was also very sandy. It was easy to track her footprints because the ground was wet and she was not wearing any shoes. I followed her footprints to a nearby village and I saw her sitting on a stool.

I could see that her face was swollen; I could not bear looking at her, she was a mess. I was crying like a wounded animal and I was inconsolable. My mother was burnt by my father, the man well known for his violence and aggressions. My mother had been hurt by the man she loved and had followed him to Zimbabwe after she had fallen in love with him. He had been working in South Africa when they met, and from my understanding, they crossed the border illegally as my mother did not have any documents to travel.

I never forgave him for what he did to my mother. I never wanted to know him thereafter. He had made me grow up very quickly, though. He believed that sending girls to school was a waste of his money, even though schools were free. He was still against the idea! He believed that boys should go to school instead, but the boys in the family let him down on several occasions. But my mind was with my mother and wondering where she was and whether she had survived; death was not on my mind yet, but I knew she was hurt, wherever she was.

There was another episode when my father was angry towards me; he started shouting and I knew there was going to be trouble. So, I began to run towards the fields for refuge, running as fast as my little feet could take me. After a while I returned home, and my mother was sitting by the shed. She told me that when she saw him pick the knobkerry up and throw it towards me, she had closed her eyes thinking that her child was going to die. But when she opened her eyes, she knew the knobkerry had missed me, as she did not see me on the floor. *Thank God she is alive,* my mother had thought. My father had missed me.

There was another time I remember when he had bought dried fish, and I was supposed to cook it, as I did the cooking for everyone. I was more grown up than my other siblings and it was one of my chores; I did the cooking by boiling the fish over the fire, but I did not know how to cook the dried fish. I was not a good cook, but those were one of the duties which I was supposed to do as a girl growing up.

I served the fish for him, but he was drunk; he was asking me a lot of questions about the fish, and he was very angry as I did not cook it to his standard. So, he grabbed me, pinned me down and then knelt on my throat. He then beat me so hard and several times using a 'sjambok'. I was screaming, and my mother was not there. I could not move my neck for weeks on end. It was excruciating! That was how bad it was. I found it exceedingly difficult to forgive him for this particular incident. I helped a lot by cooking and going to fetch firewood, but during that time there were limitations to what I could do. I could not even go and fetch water or firewood; I became crippled because of that event. I could not even do the cooking.

When the sniff was not available, he would send me to a nearby village to ask neighbours for it, as he knew who smoked this sniff. He would ask me to spit on the floor before I left and then run fast as I could—I had to be back home before the spit had dried.

He was extraordinarily strong, and villagers feared him. He loved to drink, and he was very well known for his abusive behaviour. I remember my father used to hide his money in a hole he had dug in one of the rooms, but we were all aware of it. He also enjoyed gambling, and from my understanding he would win at times. My father was very kind to the villagers, sharing beer that mostly would have been made by my mother.

I remember clearly when my father went to sell his firewood. He would sometimes buy some presents for us to bring home. It wasn't much, but one day he arrived home and asked where my sisters were. I knew of course, they were playing in the next village. Then I thought to myself, let somebody else get beaten for a change. He asked me to go and tell them that he had arrived home, so I went off to find them. I told them that he was very angry because they were not at home to greet him, and when they walked in, he was sitting on a stool, waiting for them. I remained outside and looked cautiously through the window to see what was happening, but remained vigilant, just in case he turned on me once again. But surprisingly he didn't do a thing, which shocked me. I was shocked because I came to the realisation that whatever wrong deeds my sisters did, they would never be punished like I had been. This realisation weighed heavily on my heart and was one of the contributing factors to moving out of that village.

I left the village thinking I was going to get some respite, but this turned out not be the case. I was in a different environment living with my sister; it was hers, and I needed to dance to her music. I had no other alternatives but to live with her or otherwise go back to my abusive father. In Matedzi there were so many mangoes and they used to grow in people's houses, which belonged to the railways. If you were working for the railways, you were given a house to live in rent free.

My sister's husband was one of them. Rhodesia (before after it was called Zimbabwe), was a genuinely nice place to live, and they managed to leave Matedzi and bought a house in Bulawayo. It was a big house with a servant cottage. When my mother came to visit, she would sleep on the floor in the servant cottage, but there were mosquitoes in there. After running away from my violent father, she was given a meal once a day, which was extremely difficult to watch. The house in Bulawayo was quite large, however, it had only one bathroom which we all had to share. The man whom my sister had married also had daughters from a previous marriage, who I got on well with.

One Christmas we went to a place called Lucosy Matedzi where their friends lived. But little did I know what was about to happen. After being given some alcohol, I was raped. I then left the village and went to live with my older sister, hoping that I would be safe there. I was only thirteen or fourteen years old at that time, and the sexual assault had left me pregnant. I couldn't say anything, either, as the man who raped me was married with children. I can remember filling up a tub of hot water and soaking myself in it, not knowing what to do. I was very scared and confused.

I struggled during the pregnancy with no support. I was selling beers for my sister during that time as their friend was the one who had raped me, but this was never to be spoken about. This man was married and had his own siblings, but I was told by my sister to keep my mouth shut for fear of having to return home to my father.

I was a child who was supposed to bring another child into this world, and I did not get any help. I tried to make ends meet but it was extremely difficult. The guy who raped me did not want to know, presumably in fear of losing his wife. I had a son who had no father after he had rejected him. He knew the baby was his but he denied this, and finally we had to go to court in Harare for a blood test to prove it was his son.

We had caught the same train, but he never came to say hello to his son, and I knew it would be a challenge to get child maintenance. I did not know the system at all, which was a disadvantage for me and my son. I could not say what had happened to me in fear that I might be sent back home to my abusive father. My first-born child was a boy, but I was only a child as well, and I could not look after him as a mother should. I regret that every single day. It would have been nice to say something about giving birth to my first child, but it was not to be. I had carried this pregnancy for nine months and my son was born by Caesarean section.

It was extremely difficult having to live with my elder sister. I was given the cold shoulder if I didn't wake up to clean and cook breakfast. If I didn't contribute then there would be no food on the table, and I would be left to watch the children eat. This was how my elder sister was, and I had to do all her chores before doing anything else for myself.

I did a shorthand course for a month, but this did not go far. I only managed to pay for just two months. I was very ambitious; I wanted to do something with my life, although I did not have enough money to pay the fees for my education. Due to financial difficulties, I was forced to leave college and look for a job. My friend and I found work for a band, although we were not very good at singing.

I washed clothes in the morning by hand as they did not have a washing machine, and then I would hang them outside to dry. When I finished the housework, I would prepare a full English breakfast and then there would be ironing to be done.

During my time in the band, I met a man who became my boyfriend. I used to call him my husband, even though we were not married. He had taught me how to play the drums, but I was not very good at it. Little did I know he was going to be a violent man.

We lived together in a rented flat in the city centre of Bulawayo. He used to work in Mpilo hospital. In the beginning, everything was going extremely well and nobody could separate us; he enjoyed karate as his sport and played drums in the band, and he used to do this after he finished work.

We were inseparable, and he loved me. He would want me to escort him to his karate class, and he wanted to have children. However, during that time I was not able to get pregnant. I had a son whom he refused to acknowledge, as in Africa, a man cannot bring up another man's child, something which his family would have been opposed to. So, I had to leave my son with my elder sister.

He was the breadwinner and he provided for us both. I would wash and iron his clothes. He did not speak fluent Ndebele, and at that time I could not speak Shona (his language), so I used to communicate with him in English, which I was particularly good at.

He decided that we would move back to Harare (Salisbury), which I agreed to. It was his homeland. I thought things would be okay because he was a good man, but all that was about to change. He would beat me and make it out to be my fault, yet later apologise for his actions. Then he would want to make love to me, which he would do without my consent. There were times when I could have run away from him and gone back to living with my sister, but then he would apologise, something which became a pattern in our lives together.

As I did not have any money, or any savings of my own, I would forgive him and return to the flat. If I went to the shop to buy milk, he would follow me. We had lived in the flat for a year before moving to Harare. In the beginning everything was fine. We were living with his brother and his wife who had a daughter. Their marriage was not very stable, and his brother had a mistress and would often spend days away before returning home. They both wanted more children but that was not to be.

My boyfriend got a job at Parirenyatwa Hospital, which was one of the biggest hospitals in Harare. We lived with his brother until I gave birth to my daughter by Caesarean section. We had our own bedroom and we stayed with them for more than two years, before he decided to find a place for us to live. It was a three-bedroom house; big enough to lease one of the rooms to a university graduate. The house had a big bathroom, a kitchen, a lounge, and a large garden, where I planted vegetables and flowers. Fast-forward two years later we had a son, delivered by Caesarian again.

When things were good, they were good. I remember one day he took us to a drive-in to watch a movie, but children were not allowed in so we had to turn back. But on our way home, he said that he really wanted us to go and watch this movie, so he came up with a plan. He took a small blanket from the house and covered the children in the back seat of the car. I was sitting at the front; he decided he wanted the children to watch the movie, so he drove back to the drive-in, bought popcorn, and gave it to the children. The funny part was that nobody said a thing, so we were able to watch the movie and then go back home.

But he started to womanize, making other women pregnant behind my back, coming home late, and he started to be abusive just like my father. I did not have any money, or any savings; after all, he was the breadwinner.

He hit me in front of my children, and he nearly left me for dead; in his own words, he told me he wanted to kill me, or for me to walk away from his house as a cripple, and he meant it. He used a sweeping broom to beat me. I fainted as my children were hiding in the wardrobe, and when I opened my eyes, I felt the warm feeling of my blood dripping down my face—even now I have a scar on my head. My elbows and knees were also affected by the beatings I took and at times I find it difficult to write about this as it feels like I am reliving the nightmare. To say how I got out alive was a miracle; when he was finished hitting me, he took his car and left. I did not know where he was going. I knew the time had come for me to leave and I would have to escape without my children. There was no other solution to it all.

My body was numb and my face was swollen beyond recognition. The thought of leaving my children behind was at the back of my mind. I was in a lot of pain. However, I decided to stay a bit longer, to use a window of opportunity so that when he went to work, I would pack up and take the children with me, but this did not happen.

I left the house although I had no idea where he had gone to. I wanted my children, and therefore I decided to hide next door in the chicken run. I could hear his car pull up, and all I could think about was my children and thinking of ways of taking them away from all this, regardless of the situation I was in. I remained next door, hiding in the chicken run, waiting for an opportunity to go back into the house and collect my belongings. I thought of my mother and how she would have remained with us, no matter how difficult the situation had become.

After hiding in the chicken run for some time, I heard his car pull away, so I returned to the house, looking for my children. As soon as I approached the gates, the lady who was leasing a room advised me to leave, stating that it was not safe for me to remain on the premises. I took her advice, and she took me to her small house. I left without my children or any belongings.

She took me to one of her relatives where I managed to get some sleep. The next day, I went to hospital, and when I got there, they did a scan to find out if I had any broken bones or skull damage. My body was badly beaten but it was only tissue damage. I remember leaving the hospital and a gentleman asked me what had happened. I lied and told him that I had been in a car accident. He was shocked and said, "You look so bad; did anyone survive?" I said no but knew that I had had no alternative but to leave him.

I was not talking to anyone; all I wanted was to sleep.

I was prescribed some painkillers which I picked up from the pharmacy with the little money that I had. When I returned to the accommodation, the lady squeezed some tomato juice to use as eye drops to get my eyes to clear. I slept afterwards. I was missing my children, but powerless to do anything about it.

I stayed with her for a while, but I had a brother who was in the army, and I knew if I went to see him, he would be able to give me money to travel back to Bulawayo. So, I managed to travel to the army barracks. When I saw him, he took me to the local canteen to talk. I covered my head with a scarf as I didn't want an audience. He looked at me and immediately got angry. He asked me whether my husband was at home, but I was uncertain of his whereabouts. My brother Keith said that if he knew he was at home he would go and shoot him in cold blood. He was so angry, whereas I was numb, and all what I really wanted was my children. I knew it would be so difficult to get them, but they were my children and they needed me. I was done with crying. I had nothing, neither clothes nor underpants. I had left with nothing.

My brother had said to me that this reminded him of Tina Turner and Ike: *Tina finally managed to escape her abusive husband one night when he fell asleep, grabbing a toiletry bag and running, narrowly missing a truck as she dashed across a highway. With just 36 cents in her pocket, she pleaded with the owner of an inn to let her stay.* She said: "I was running towards a new life." – Tina Turner.

My brother lived in Harare and was a pilot in the army. With the money that he gave me I was able to board a train back to Bulawayo. I didn't have a job but knew that I had to look for some accommodation and raise enough money to be able to return to Harare and collect my children. The swelling had gone down and I felt better physically, so having reached Bulawayo, I started to search for various jobs and some accommodation. I managed to find a room to rent; it was very small, not at all clean, but finally I had a roof over my head. A place where I could stay without any violence or being used as a punch bag.

I briefly lived with relatives, but it was not the same without my children. I missed them very much and not a day passed by without me wondering who was cooking for them, if had they had a bath and if they wearing clean clothes.

I contacted the Bulawayo law courts. It was the only way to get my children back, and I did it. I travelled to the police station in Harare, and on arriving at the house where we lived, he was not there. I was informed that he had gone to his brother's house, so we drove there with the police, but we were informed that he was in prison and my children had been taken to his village in Rusape. I knew where his parents lived but his mother did not like me that much as I was from Matabeleland and he was from Harare. They had their cultural differences and their way of doing things was completely different from what I was used to. I needed to travel back to Bulawayo, which meant leaving my children in Harare. I had no choice but to leave, with the goal that I would return one day and collect them. I was determined to do so, but little did I know then that I was pregnant.

He was in prison and refused to sign the court papers, denying that it was him they were looking for. I still had serious money issues and I would have to find a job somehow if I wanted to my children back. I would do whatever it took to make that happen.

I wanted my children with me. I knew I was going to be difficult, and it was a journey I was willing to take. When I left the hospital, they told me to go and get pills from the pharmacy, but I did not have any or money to buy them so I returned to the house with an intent to get my children. He made me sleep in the spare bedroom. He still wanted to hit me; threats were made during this time claiming we wanted to kill me before I left him and I really thought he was going to do that. I was scared and a mess. I was already sleeping in the spare bedroom but I did not know what he was going to do next. My hope wasthat if he left for work I would get the children and leave.

Another trip this time, and I was with my sister who volunteered to come, and my children were sent to his home village in Rusape to live with his parents as he was serving a jail sentence. I went to the Rusape police station with my late sister, who was overhelpful, and tried to help me get my children when we attended the village. I was escorted by the Rusape policemen and found my daughter outside the village doing dishes; it was so cold, and we all sat in the village kitchen where my mother-in-law was with her husband. She started shouting at me with no reason, calling me nasty names under the sun. My son became very restless, walking up and down whilst the police tried to talk to my in-laws, but when I set my eyes on my daughter, she was calm.

My mother-in-law was not happy, she tried to refuse to give me my children and the police had to do their job. My father-in-law was silent at first and then said, "Wherever my grandchildren are going, I am also coming with them." He was allowed to travel with us in the police van and came to the police station with us. Nobody said anything in the police van, and I had my children and my late sister who travelled with me. I miss my sister so much; she passed away at such a young age and had a gentle soul. She was very kind. My mother-in-law had been abusive and directed a lot of foul language at me, blaming me for her son being in prison, and my sister didn't understand why I didn't say anything back to her. But all I wanted was to have my children back.

When we left the village, my mother-in-law refused to give me my children's clothes, so we left with what they were wearing. At the police station, my father-in-law was told this was as far as he could come, and that I was taking the kids with me. We were so lucky; as soon as we got to the railway station, the train to Bulawayo was just about to leave, so we boarded the train with my kids with no shoes or jumpers on their backs. My daughter's hands were cracked through washing dishes in the cold weather; it was heart breaking, but I had comfort knowing that they were now with me.

It was very cold on the train, so I took my jumper off and gave it to my daughter, and my son was given a jumper from my young sister. We were heading back to Bulawayo and I wanted to give them the best education, which I did not have. I wanted to empower them by providing them with a good school. Jobs were difficult to find, and life was hard.

We managed to keep them warm on the train, but it was very cold, and when we finally arrived at Bulawayo, we stayed with my other sister who had bought a house with reasonable room. But things did not go very well there. My kids were accused of breaking door handles, and not in a nice way; after all my children had gone through, that hurt me. My sister asked me to move to the servants' quarters, and memories came flooding back to when my other elder sister did the same to my mother.

This place had a bad stench to it and I tried to clean it. There was no electricity and we had to use candles, but I had my children with me this time and had found them a primary school nearby. I had managed to secure a job, too, at a hotel, which was just walking distance from where we were staying.

I believed my relatives would help in looking after the children, but I was wrong. My sister came back from Germany and decided to buy a big house and she wanted most of her siblings to come and live with her; fortunately, I was one of them, and my sister knew about my situation. There was a time when my sister did not have any accommodation, where she lived with me in this small rented room where I was living and she had arrived from overseas. She had encouraged me to go to Harare and bring the children with me, as now she had a big house, and everything would be okay.

I know other people want their children to go through what they went through, which I find difficult to understand. I tried to make sure my children came first, and I knew they loved me, and I am a proud mother. It was not easy during this time to support them single-handedly. I didn't get support from anyone, I had to rely on myself to clothe and feed us.

I was living with my children in Bulawayo where I got a job as a chambermaid in a very expensive hotel, which is where Morgan Freeman was staying while he was over in

Zimbabwe making a movie. He gave me a tip of ten dollars. I had seen him on TV, and I was ecstatic to see him and the crew. He was so nice to me, and he shook my hand.

When they arrived from America, Warner Brothers booked into a hotel called Nesbitt Castle, which is one of the most expensive hotels in Bulawayo. I met with Keith, who also was travelling with Warner Brothers and was an artist for them. They used to leave early in the morning for castings and I used to clean his room and make his bed every day. He used to leave notes in our secret places and used to tell me what time they would come back after casting.

Before they left, he asked me join him in America and I was willing to go but it turned out not to be as when Warner Brothers left, I did not hear from him.

Although there were not many rooms, they needed to be spotlessly clean. We were allocated rooms to clean and these rooms were all given names; all the bedrooms had brass taps and they had to be cleaned thoroughly. It was hard and during that time we were not given any lunch. The money was not good. I had already heard that in South Africa there were better paying jobs, but I had to think of the children, and I worried about who was going to look after them when I was not there. The decision to go to South Africa was not an easy one. But I went anyway with the hope to raise more money.

South Africa

Despite the prospect of poor wages, I made the decision to go to South Africa. I did not have a passport, but I knew it could be done even though there were risks involved. I would make the journey on the bus with a man I knew from church, which would take us as close as the border, and then make the rest of the journey on foot when it got dark. By the time we reached the border there were three of us ready to make the rest of the trip together; we would have to cross the Limpopo River to get into South Africa, which was extremely difficult.

The man from Zimbabwe who was travelling with us had some knowledge of the journey we had to take, but we had little money to get us there. I remember the journey very clearly; it was early morning, and we were going to cross the border illegally as we had no travel documentation. As we began to cross the river, suddenly, behind us, two big elephants started charging after me. They were making a very loud noise and their ears were flapping as they moved towards me. There was nothing I could do but to hope that the danger would pass.

The three of us scattered in different directions. Although I used to be a fast runner as a child, this was a completely different ballgame—my life was in danger. The men were much quicker than me, and I soon found myself on my own, so I decided to try and find a place to hide until the danger had passed. I managed to push my way through the water and hide out at the root of a tree and hanging branches, where I was hanging on for dear life, my heart beating hard against my chest.

The elephants came closer, still making that noise, but I held on tight. I did not make a sound for fear of my life. I could see them beyond the branches where I lay low. I had been left on my own and now I was fighting for survival. This was just the beginning of a difficult journey.

When the danger finally passed and the elephants moved on to drink further up the river, I came out from the safety of the branches and started to make my way across the river. When I got to the other side, the two men were there waiting for me, but they were shocked that I had made it across safely. The journey should have been made during the night, but at least we had finally made it across the border.

Early the next morning we were introduced to our boss and then given our duties of going to the fields to pick potatoes. A van would pick us up and take us out onto the fields; there would be many of us, men, women and children doing the same job. We had been given a room too, which was full of bed bugs, and I was covered in bite marks. We didn't have any money, but we were allowed to get credit from the local shop to buy food, which would then be deducted from our wages. These were very demanding working conditions; the potatoes were picked and then put into bags and weighed. It was hard work, especially during the intense heat of the day. There were many people who had been doing this for a long time, and I wondered how they had managed to do so. It was extremely difficult, working long hours throughout each day, but I managed to do it.

I made sure I was able to save enough money, buying only the most essential of items. I worked on the farm for two months, and during this time of hard labour, I had little clothing to wear. I only had one long skirt, and I had lost a lot of weight during that time. I was struggling, but I knew I had to remain strong.

After two months I eventually left the farm with a view of travelling further this time, to the city of Johannesburg, to try and get a job there. Again, with no money it was not easy; it was like climbing Mount Kilimanjaro with no equipment. I swallowed before chewing my food, which has made me to be the person that I am today. I have made mistakes, which I have realised and learned from. Life is not easy when you have children and are a single parent, but I love them all, regardless of what they have done, in the past and present.

I always thought about my children back in Zimbabwe, and wondered if they were still going to school. Did they wonder where I was? I had no way of contacting them, and the pain of not being with them was unbearable. It felt like I was in prison! But I had to keep going, for their sakes, and only hoped that they were safe and still under my sister's care.

I discovered soon after that this was not the case. When I finally contacted my children, I was informed that they had been sent to my home village, and they could not speak the Ndebele language. There was only my mother who they could turn to, and she didn't know them that well.

That was very painful for me. I felt let down by my sister and could only wonder what would have happened to them if I had died while trying to cross the Limpopo River. I was a single parent with very little income, but I knew I had to pick myself up if I was ever to see them again.

My son explained to me how difficult it was for him being pulled out of school by my sister when he had been doing so well in sports and enjoying swimming lessons. When I heard about this, it pained me very much. I was also concerned about their wellbeing; they were my children, and I loved them very much and had gone through such an ordeal to get them away from their father.

I knew to try and contact them would be extremely hard as I did not have a phone; it was very tough as I wanted to let them know I was still okay. At this farm there were no phones to contact loved ones and not only that, when one returned to the farm at night, one would always be extremely tired.

As I wanted money to travel further were, I was Getting a job unlike where we were, told it will be easier which we not as hard as picking up potatoes the whole day for just little bit of money. We worked hard in those conditions, any.

prior to getting this farm we discussed move forward this was the plan there fore we worked hard and as soon as the end of that month it will be time to move further,as much we could this was challenge. There was also one of the guys who also had the same plan, after meeting him in this farm and now were where three as there also was these men who we met by the farm, and he also wanted to go to Jonesburg burg End of the month. This journey was the survival of the fittest and I was not one of them, but I had a purpose live for my kids

Once we had managed to raise enough money, the plan was to progress further, and we maintained this; we counted every penny once we got paid. Having said our morning prayers, we then paid the local shopkeeper what we owed, we left the farm and were on our way to Johannesburg. We had left during the early hours of the morning and we travelled light, without mobile phones and with very little clothing.

It was blazing hot, and we had brought no water on the journey. We were all very thirsty indeed. Once we reached the river, we stopped so we could get out and take a drink. I could hear animals nearby, but I was not afraid. The water was dirty and full of animal droppings, which we tried to push out of the way before taking a drink. But we were so thirsty, we had no option but to drink the water.

Suddenly, a jeep pulled up nearby and gunfire was heard. A white man sat in the driving seat while a Boer got out and shot at men who were running away. I put my hands up to signal my surrender; I was fearing for my life, thinking that he was going to shoot me.

He ordered me to sit in the back of his jeep, which had no canopy, and he drove extremely fast. There was a dog sitting up front, but the driver did not look at all friendly. After driving for some time, he pulled over into a garage. He was speaking Afrikaans, and I could barely understand what he was saying to me.

He pointed at my skirt and told me to pull it down. I did as he told me and I could see that he knew I was very scared. I was like a mouse that had seen a cat, and I wondered if he was going to shoot me. I had lost so much weight and I was on my period, but that was the least of my worries at that time. He drove me to the police station, and he left me there. At that particular time, I did not even ask him for water although I was very thirsty. I was told to sit down while the policemen took a statement from me. I asked for a drink of water, which they gave me, although I struggled to understand what they were talking about. They were speaking a language I didn't understand, and I could only wonder what was going to happen to me.

My mind was racing in different directions. I knew I had to get out of there. I could see wired fences around the perimeter, presumably to keep the wild animals at bay. I was trying to figure out how to make my escape and wondered if I could mae it out of there and run far enough until I was able to hide. I wasn't sure. Time was ticking by, and it was starting to get dark.

I had asked to use the toilet and for more water, and as I looked at the clock on the wall, I wondered how long it would be until they finished their shift.

I went to the toilet for a second time and I remember making a short prayer to the Lord, to be with me. I washed my hands and face and knew that the time had come for me to leave. I was thinking of my children and the time I had spent without them all the while I was on the farm picking up potatoes. I had no intention of going back there, so this was a risk I was willing to take. I was willing to take my own life and I was no longer afraid.

I ran out of the building and on to gravel road, running away as fast as I could. I lost one of my shoes, but just kept on running until I found a place safe enough to hide. I discovered some thorn bushes away from the police station and hid there, hoping that they would not find me.

I saw one of the policemen walk past me. He was on his walkie-talkie, presumably asking for back up, but eventually he turned back to his car and drove away. I remained hidden in the bushes and it was later when they drove by again, using a search light to look for me; it was getting dark, but I remained where I was, lying still until they drove away.

I lay low until it was dark and then decided to make my

escape. I only had one shoe, and I had to walk on stones and thorns. But to get out of there I had to get beyond the barbed wire fencing. I walked for hours trying to find a way out, but the perimeter was heavily guarded with wire and impossible for me to climb over.

I ran, I heard calls, sirens but I kept running, but I did not even look, but amazingly enough I just dived down where there was thorns and I looked for a place just to hide and I did hold my breath, and

I was lying down, but I was not taking any chances, I really wanted to be sure, therefore I stayed down. Until it was slightly dark, and I wanted to make sure the police have gone, from where I was hiding, they made few trips before giving up, now I was on my own, and thought how was I going to move with one shoe, there was a thought that crossed my mind during that time to try and find my other shoe will I be able to travel to the unknow land with one shoe. But deep down I knew that was not an opinion my chances of survival were running very slim. I remember seeing tress.

I was going around in circles, worried that they might see me. It was so dark and I was finding it difficult to see. I searched for many hours for a way out, and eventually I discovered an area below the fencing and started to dig using my bare hands. I pulled away at the dirt to allow a small gap that would allow me to get through. As I dragged myself under the fence, my skirt and legs were being caught on the barbed wire, but I just kept on going until finally I broke free.

The sun was starting to rise as I got to my feet, and so I started on my way. I was walking with only one shoe, and now there was the added danger of wild animals that could be lurking, but I had lost all fear. I was tired and thirsty, but I just kept on moving forward in the hope that I would reach a farm or meet someone who could help me. I kept thinking of my children, which was enough to keep me going.

Suddenly, a man appeared out of nowhere. I thought I was beginning to hallucinate. As I got closer to him, I could see he was an old man, who was speaking to me in a language I did not understand. I made sign language to demonstrate my thirst, and he gave me a cup of water and then led me away to safety. Darkness had fallen again by the time we had reached his village, but he offered me a place to rest. I slept on the floor, but that did not bother me, I was just so tired and exhausted from the journey.

I vaguely remember him telling me that I was safe, and that he would try and escort me to where I could find transport that would allow me to travel further. He also had a relative who would help me get some shoes.

I spent a week with this man and in the safety of his home. He said he would help me get a lift to Johannesburg and I was able to get some blue shoes. I ate some mincemeat with one of the families in the village, which gave me a terrible stomachache, but I was able to pull myself together for the journey ahead.

On arrival in South Africa, I found some housekeeping jobs; the money was not good, which was why I had to work several jobs (some part time). I had a room to sleep in and I found that I could go and do ironing for other people, which is the reason I am very good at ironing today. At times I would find piles of clothes that needed to be ironed and I could do that just to get bit of money. I made the decision to send my children to a boarding school, which was awfully expensive.

One of the employees left South Africa and went to Europe with her husband and two children (a girl and a boy). They were genuinely nice, and she is the lady who made me realise that there was more that I could do even though I did not have much education. She advised me to do a lot of coursework, e.g., cooking, or full-time childminding. I did those courses and then I started to look for other jobs when she left, but things were not the same anymore. I was missing her family so much as they had been so good to me. She was the one who had bought me a plane ticket to fly to Zimbabwe, as she wanted me to feel how it was to fly.

There was a promise of another job, which again she had helped me with by introducing me to this family. The lady had twins and she was looking for a nanny to look after her children when she visited England with her husband. Presumably they had money, and I had agreed on return from Zimbabwe after visiting my children.

I had only been gone for less than a month when the plans were changed. I was not going to go to England anymore; my dreams were shattered by my employer, who knew before I had returned, and she passed on the news to me. I was devastated; this news was overwhelming.

I could not believe it, but I had to start looking for another job as soon as possible, and I got one. At the same time, there we are flitting thoughts in my mind; I had to try and make it on my own for the sake of my children, as now they were in a boarding school, which meant I had to take everything. I did have money, but the money that I was getting paid, I used to pay for the children's boarding school. It was difficult to save money after that, so I sold everything I had, including my bed, which I sacrificed to sleep on the floor.

I had seen an advert for a job in Greece. I contacted the lady advertising the position; however, I received no support from my friends, claiming that this lady would use me by way of prostitution, but my mind was made up and I was set to move.

My journey to Greece from South Africa was another experience. I wanted to raise money to send home for the children's education as they were in a boarding school. When I was in South Africa, my mother's land, I got different jobs as a domestic worker and at times working as babysitter, as it was not difficult to get a job there.

I needed to find a job desperately, but I knew if I looked hard enough, I would find one. I began my search by knocking on white people's doors looking for work. I had sisters who lived and worked abroad, so I felt that a move was the right thing to do.

Greece

I arrived at the Greek airport after such an agonising trip. I was exhausted and very confused. I did not know where we were going, and we arrived at 7 pm instead of 8 pm. I saw people who were standing with tags which had people's names written on them. I supposed it was for those people that arrived that day with us, for them to know who they were with and where they were going.

It was extremely hot, and although I am used to hot weather, the weather was more humid. I was introduced to the family that I was going to assist as a housemaid, and they were kind. I met the current housekeeper, and she was from Philippines, and was also nice to me. By now, though, I was tired and very hungry.

I was shown a small room where I was going to sleep, and wondered how long I would be staying here. The room and window were so small it would drive me mad. I was given supper, which had chicken and fish, which my sister used to cook. I ate it all up and enjoyed it very much. I feared the uncertainty, though. This was a new place, new surroundings. I knew little of the family that had taken me on, and what they thought of me as I was black and from Africa.

It was extremely hot. The family had another carer, a Filipino, who had arrived in the morning. I was already up by that time. I followed her all over like a dog following its master. I wanted to learn a lot of things during this time. I envied her knowledge and I decided this was my time to put in everything I knew, everything that I had learned in the past. I knew this was the time to learn from her and put everything in good use. I was confused still, but not missing the family that much. I had a job, therefore I needed to concentrate if I really wanted this to work out for me, and I did. I knew what I was doing was for my children back home. This needed to be done, and I was going to focus on my job and see it through.

I knew there would be little contact with family for a while.

On my second day I slept like a baby, and in the morning I had a shower, and then I joined the family. This was when I met their only son; they were a grown couple, and only had one child. I introduced myself and at least he could speak back to me in English. I was hoping to get along with him, as he appeared to be the apple of their eyes. I wondered what this boy thought of me, presumably I was very anxious as I did not want to make any mistakes.

Later that same day I met up with two ladies after doing all the house chores. We went to the market, and I watched how Greek people sold their products. My thoughts raced back to the market in South Africa, where normally this job was done by black women or men. I realised that there were many differences in culture and lifestyle. Also, one thing that stuck in mind was how small the streets and houses were. I felt like I was starting to let my guard down.

That week went by with little change. I was thinking more about my children, though. I knew I was alone, but I knew if things got bad, I had bought a return ticket and could always return home. But I was not going to go back that easily, as I knew I would struggle if I returned. I had to try harder, but it was so difficult for me.

My mind was racing, but I reminded myself that I am a God-fearing person, and I did believe he was going to forsake me, my belief was strong. This time I prayed, I thought of my children back home. I was given the news that the other carer was admitted to hospital as she was extremely sick.

I wished I was back in South Africa. I felt useless that I did not have any control of my life. At the same time, I felt like an open book. I did not make any decisions as everything was decided for me. I felt the humiliation. I felt empty and there were so many questions going through my mind. So many thoughts and questions, all of which I had no answer to. It was a scary situation and I felt helpless to do anything about it. I had an upset stomach, and the Filipino lady remained in hospital.

I knew deep down that this was not the job that I had travelled so far to do. I needed to come up with a decision quickly. I was not even familiar with Greece. I had just arrived, and I didn't really know anyone. It seemed my best bet was try and speak to the Filipino when she came out of hospital and to ask for her help. It was my only way forward. And this was a good decision for me as she had been to Greece for a very long time and so was familiar with her surroundings. And not only that, she would know places I could go if I wanted a job. She mentioned that I was welcome to live with her and her sister until I found a job, so I packed my bags and left.

I stayed with this lady and her family while I got myself another job. I worked for a family who had a business in the city centre and travelled with them to work in their car.

However, it wasn't long before I got myself another job for a family whose children were grown up and seldom at home. This was in a three-storey house near the sea, with en-suite bathroom and huge lounge and bedrooms. The family had decided to go on holiday, and I had to go along with them.

We were going on holiday to a place called ~~Speeks;~~ and while it was different to anything I was used to, I was happy being on the island. I was like a child in a candy shop. The holiday spirit was high, and the son was spoiled rotten.

We went to another island in July called Kifissia and the family drove to one of the seaports. We passed through a place their friend lived as she was going to join us. The lady had two boys, and suddenly, the car became crowded, although it was one of those fancy Land Rovers.

We arrived at the seaport about midday, and again we met another friend of theirs. I was not informed about her and I assumed there was no need to be, after all, I was a worker, although it would have been nice to have been introduced. After a while I knew her name; it was KP. Her husband was an old man, and they had a dog called Dani, which was small and loud.

I found most of the Greek men loved young women, as their wives looked younger. Although I did not meet the other woman's husband, everything was okay. We boarded a ship called The Dolphin for the first time and everyone was speaking the Greek language; we were all inside this ship and it was like being on an aeroplane. I sat next to one of their friends next to the window. I was surprised because it was not as fast as I expected, but we moved, and people looked relaxed. I was the only black girl on the ship, which did not bother me. If you wanted you could go and stand by the balcony, where many people would go to smoke or just take in the view. It was breathtaking. I could see everything. I felt terribly humbled by this experience, although the thought of my children lingered on. I was at sea for the very first time. It was so blue, and I had never seen so much water in my entire life.

I was very quiet as I stood on the balcony, but it just got too crowded, as most people on deck were smokers, and I did not like that. I was a non-smoker. I went back to my seat to rest for a while, but it was too noisy as there were many children around.

We had one more stop and it was in Spitzes, and it was terribly hot. We sat and had lunch, so I ordered spaghetti, which turned out to be delicious. The children were a handful, though, and I knew that I would be afforded little time to rest. I was there to work after all, not as their friend.

We got off the boat and waited for a taxi, but there were only two taxis that operated on the island. This was due to the hills and narrow roads, so much of the transport was by way of horses or motorbikes.

One of their friends was unable to walk far because she had a stitch. She was moving very slowly, which made me wonder why she had come here at all.

The family could not hire a horse, which I would have loved to have experienced, so we had to walk up the hill to where we were supposed to be staying. It was so hot; we passed a few small houses before we finally arrived at our destination. It had been a difficult walk up the hill in extreme temperatures, and while people always say that hot temperatures shouldn't bother me due to coming from a hot continent, this was noticeably different, as there was no breeze, and it was very humid.

It was a nice house and comfortable, with two bedrooms. I believe one of the bedrooms was for their son, but he been left behind as he had gone to visit his grandparents. The bedroom had two single beds and there was a beautiful view of the sea from the window. For some reason, one of their friends had brought a coat. I didn't ask why.

The parents had the main room, and the children were left to the other bedroom, which meant that I would sleep on the two-seater sofa.

The window in the room would not open, however, and the noise from the children made it very difficult for me to rest. In the end I volunteered to sleep downstairs in a room that had a double bed and built-in wardrobes. All the floors were tiled, and it was home and a life that I could easily have fallen in love with.

It was hot and humid, but there were times when the wind would be blowing. Downstairs there was the kitchen and dining room, with a room full of their pictures. It was well organised throughout.

The sitting room had a bigger sofa so I was happy to sleep there, and I could sit outside next to the swimming pool. I wanted to swim but I was nervous, considering it had been many years since I had been swimming. The Greeks loved to have an afternoon nap, something I could not do although I wanted to. After all, I was working, and not on holiday. The pay was not that good, though better than what I was getting in South Africa.

I eventually left this family and met up with the Filipino lady that was in hospital. She took me to her flat where she was living with her sister, but I did not stay with them for a long time. In Greece, jobs were not difficult to find, and I got another job and stayed there for another year. I missed my children so much, and not only that, but my sister who I had been sending money to for the children to go to boarding school, had passed away, so I was forced to return home from Greece.

It was nice to see my children once again, though only for a brief time, but at least I knew that they were safe. Children are better off living with their parents, but sadly this was not the case for me. I had to be the breadwinner, and therefore I needed to work to keep them in boarding school.

The time had come for me to leave my children once again. I had money that I had saved while working in Greece, so I was ready to begin my journey once more. This was a difficult time for me, but I wanted to give my children the best that I was able to provide.

Such is my maternal bond, after working for a year in 1998 I decided to return to Zimbabwe to see them, as I was missing them very much. They were now in various boarding schools. If my mother was still alive, she would have been very proud of me.

I have achieved so much, and I have managed to buy a house in Oxford which I call mine.

To you my mother, will you rest in peace, and you will never be forgotten by me.

My mother with her son-in-law David, at home by the village

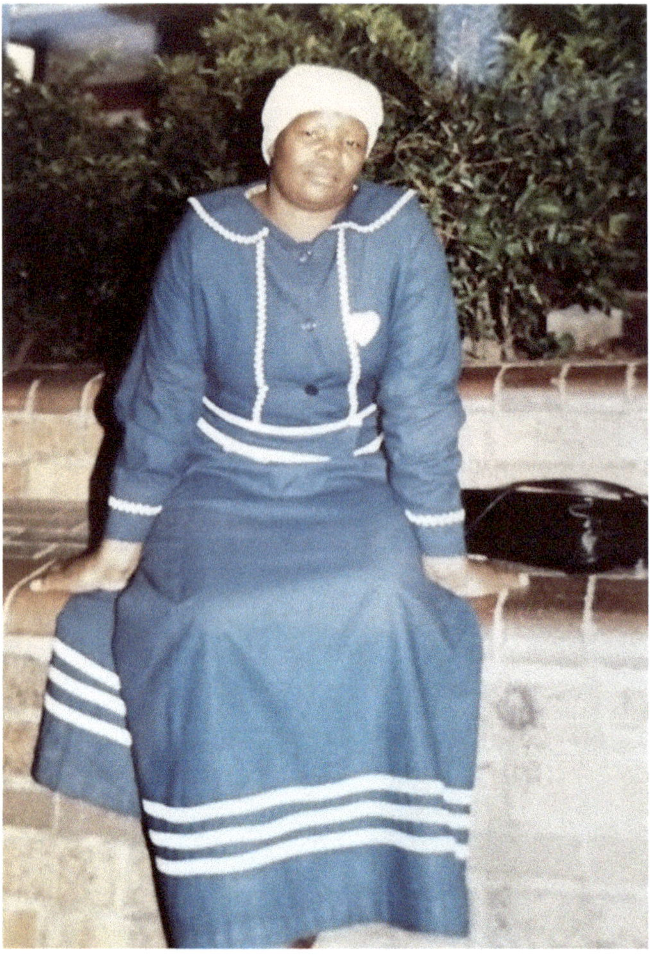

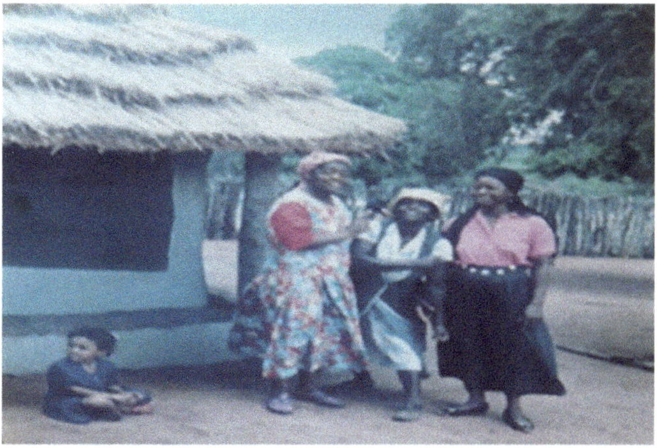

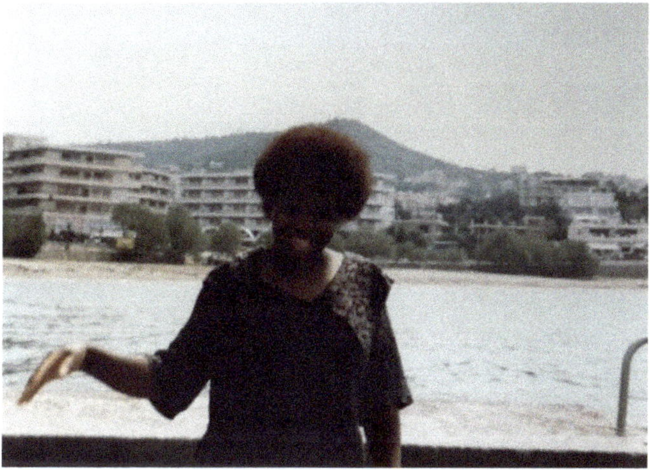

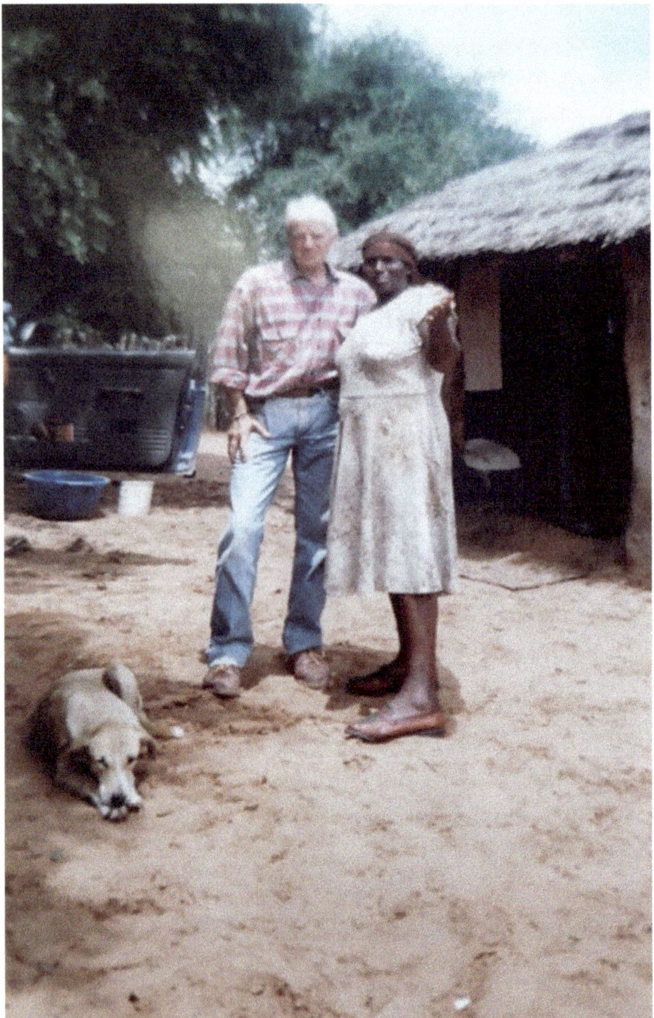

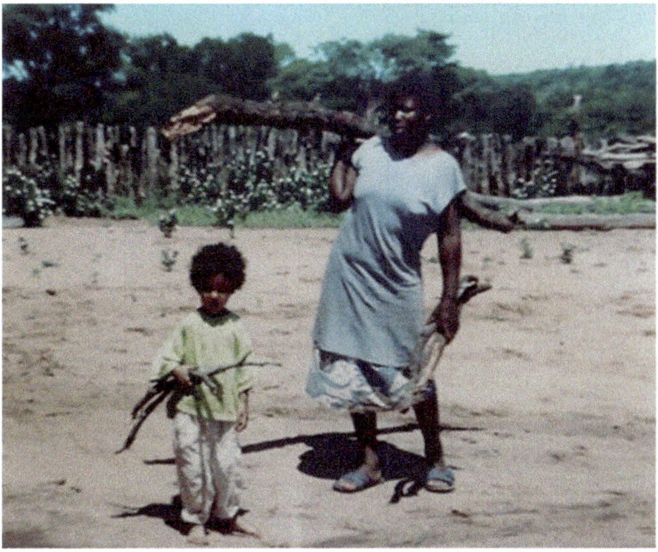

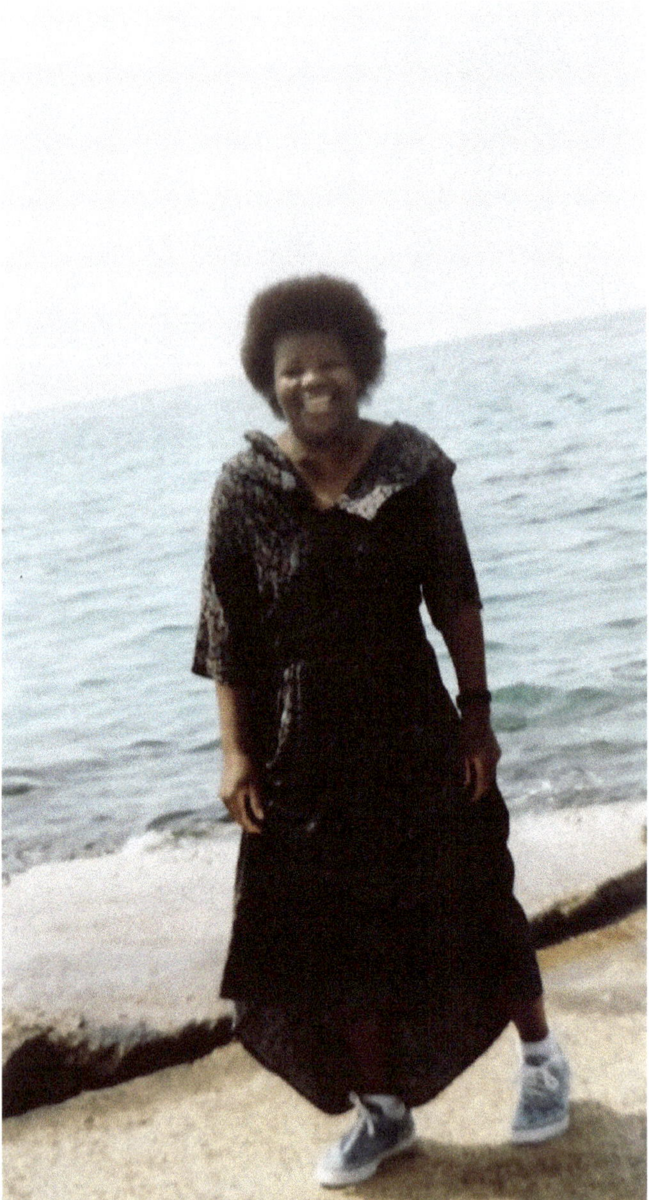

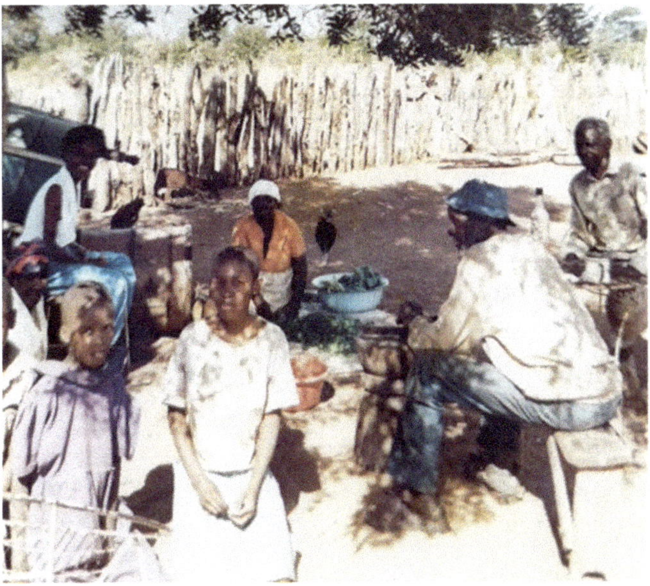

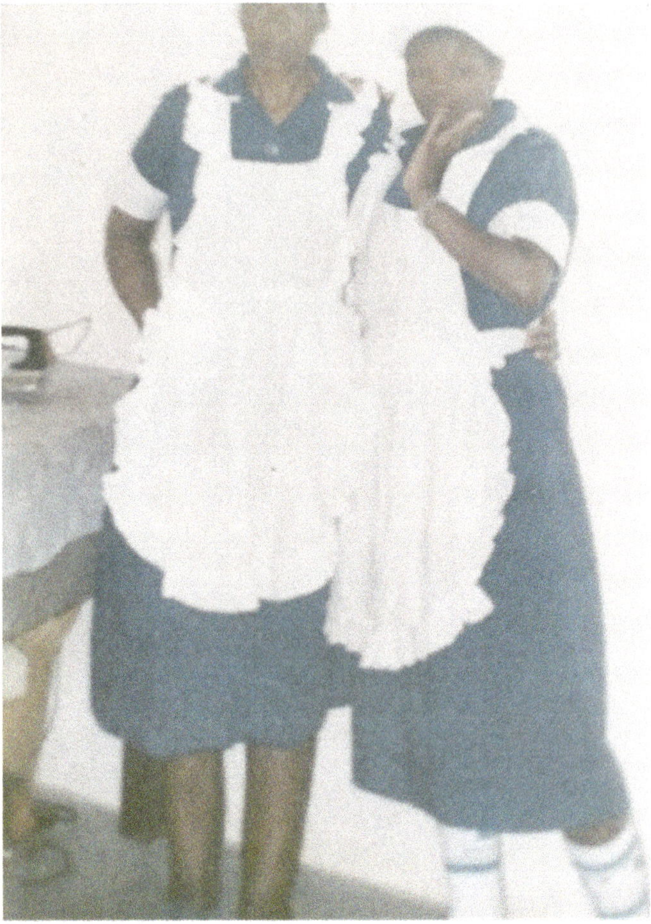

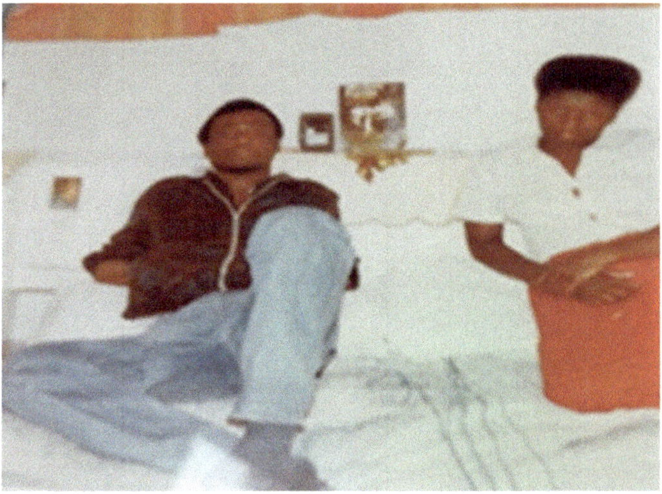

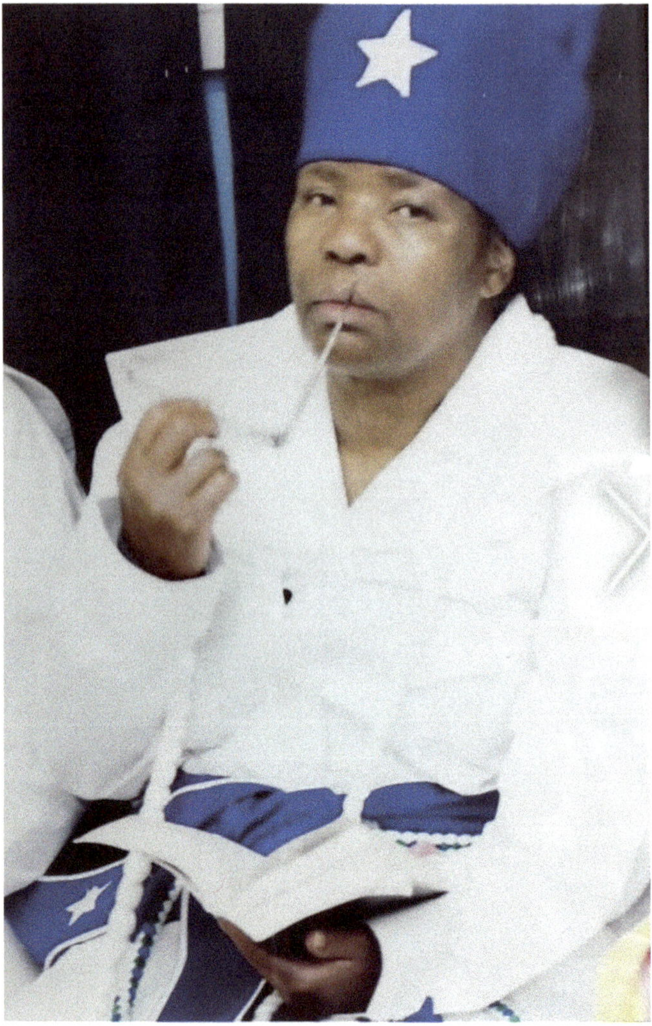

Milton Keynes UK
Ingram Content Group UK Ltd.
UKHW050309010823
426090UK00001B/3